INTIMACY
WITH
CHRIST

by
Jeanne Guyon

Her Letters Now in
Modern English

Printed in the United States

The SeedSowers
P. O. Box 3317
Jacksonville, FL 32206

Visit our exciting website at: www.seedsowers.com

Contact us by e-mail at books@seedsowers.com

ISBN 0-940232-36-7

Library of Congress Catalog Card Number 89-63686

INTIMACY
WITH
CHRIST

Formerly titled: Guyon Speaks Again

OTHER BOOKS
by
Jeanne Guyon

The Autobiography of Jeanne Guyon
Experiencing the Depths of Jesus Christ
Final Steps in Christian Maturity
Intimacy with Christ
Spiritual Torrents
Union with God

COMMENTARIES ON THE BIBLE

Genesis
Exodus
Leviticus - Numbers - Deuteronomy
Judges
Song of Songs
Jeremiah
James - I John - Revelation

Contents

Correspondence Between Jeanne Guyon and Francois Fenelon

An Essay

Foreword

Jeanne Guyon will be your counsellor through these letters which she wrote to believers who had asked her advice. This is counselling that is truly Christian, in a more Christ-centered perspective than is usually found in our present-day concept of Christian counselling.

In her letters Guyon shares with you the best on how to live the Christian life as you relate vertically with the Lord. In many of her letters she shares precious gems on relating with other believers and with the world.

If some of her language is unfamiliar to you, read her *Experiencing the Depths of Jesus Christ*. You may also want to read *Union With God* and perhaps *Spiritual Torrents*, though the first two titles are definitely recommended. All are by the same author and this publisher.

Preface

There once was a period in church history when correspondence between individuals constituted most of our literature. Books came in second. Correspondence literature has virtually vanished. Nevertheless, some of the greatest literature ever known has been found in correspondence between individuals in bygone eras. Certainly two of the greatest authors of correspondence literature in history were Jeanne Guyon and Francois Fenelon. Their letters will remain immortal as long as, from time to time, they are modernized.

Some of the most helpful material in existence on the subject of a Christian's spiritual life is found in these pages and in the correspondence literature of Fenelon.

Two hundred years from now, let us hope that someone else will put these letters in the language of their day. But for now, we are the stewards of the day we live in; and it is for this reason that this publishing house has placed these letters into modern English.

May they serve well in aiding you in your walk with Jesus Christ.

The Publishers

Introduction

I recently visited France and there traced the footsteps of Jeanne Guyon's nearly 70 years of life. As I reflect on where this compilation of her writings was penned, the thought fills me with awe. Whatever else might be said of this woman, she led a very dramatic life.

Some of her writings were penned from her home in Paris, others were written in Switzerland. Some resulted from experiences she had while under house arrest in a convent; other writings may have been penned from St. Cyr at the height of her popularity. It is possible a few were written from the dungeon of Vincennes; one letter written during a period of incarceration was even written in her own blood. (Although this letter exists today in the Archives of Paris, it is virtually unreadable.) It is doubtful that any of her correspondence written from the Bastille survived.

Her letters were written to the great, the near great, the obscure and the unknown. Some of her writings are vague, a few defy understanding, some are clear, and some lift you to the heavens. The contents of a few of her writings can literally curl the hair of an evangelical. She was, first of all, a Roman Catholic. Today she would be amazed to find herself so popular and so well received among non-Catholics.

Many Christians are very curious about how many books Guyon wrote and how many are available.

She wrote her autobiography throughout most of her life up until her imprisonment. It is generally considered to be one of the most arresting autobiographies ever penned by a Christian. It is also difficult for anyone but a Frenchman to follow. Names and places which have no meaning to most readers cause a Frenchman's mouth to drop open. Guyon crossed paths or swords with some of the greatest names of France's golden age.

Her other great work, *Experiencing the Depth of Jesus Christ,* was written in Grenoble, France about 1685. Until this day it remains one of the truly great pieces of Christian literature of all time.

Union with God is a companion edition to *Experiencing the Depths of Jesus Christ.* The place of its authorship is unknown to me. Later she penned *Spiritual Torrents,* probably the least practical of her best known books, as it is a spiritual autobiography.

Her work *A Mystical Commentary of the Bible* is very uneven, probably because it was written in haste and in an escalating atmosphere of tension. Some of it is quite beautiful, other parts lack quite a bit. Mostly it communicates how central Christ was in her thoughts.

After Guyon and her writings fell under the wrath of Louis XIV, she wrote a book entitled *Justifications* in which she explained her teachings, proved—at least to her satisfaction—that she was teaching only what Catholic mystics of the past had taught, and even commented on their commentaries. This work was never widely read and has never been translated into English.

Interestingly, she once wrote a pamphlet explaining what she was talking about in *Experiencing the Depths of Jesus Christ.* I have never seen this booklet, even in French, nor do I know of its existence. I did not knowingly run across it, even in the Archives of Paris.

The poems and letters of Jeanne Guyon span her lifetime. Her poems have always been enjoyed by Christians and a few were even set to music. Her letters, too, were a favorite for perhaps a century.

Personally, I read Guyon because I am stirred and challenged. Her eccentricities I ignore, the categorization of her teachings I leave to scholars (who fare no better than the rest of us in coming to any kind of consensus on the place of her life and teachings in church history).

I trust you will enjoy these writings and be arrested by a woman who saw Jesus Christ in virtually every circumstance of life.

Gene Edwards

General Correspondence

1

Let Christ Reign Within You

It makes me happy to see Jesus Christ inwardly reigning in the heart of one of God's children. Thank you for your good letter.

An external religion, with its rules and forms, has taken the place of an inward experience with Christ. The saints of old—Abraham, Isaac, Jacob, Enoch and Job—knew and experienced God inwardly in a personal and vital way. For Christ to truly reign within you everything must be submitted to Him without reservation. There are many who oppose such a total surrender to this reign.

Many pray, "Thy will be done on earth as it is in heaven," but have no intention of giving up their own ways, nor of allowing the cross to deal with their most deeply held desires. God wants to take each one of us, although we naturally resist it, through a desert time of experiencing the cross. He does not want to make it hard on us for no reason, but only so that we might enter the quiet *rest* of the promised land with Him.

Many refuse His call, choosing what they think to be an easier path by "going back to Egypt." They are really only going back to the slavery of their own desires. You see, most people would rather suffer anything than to allow themselves to be dethroned in the kingdom of their own heart.

It is a common idea that Jesus Christ will come again one day and reign over the entire earth. But we should ask, "Who speeds His return by giving up to His reign everything within them, here and now?"

The Lord gave you no strict rituals to follow. He teaches you to "enter into your closet," that is, to quiet yourself, open your heart, and without many words, to touch your Lord who is within you.

The Sabbath is not just a day of outward rest, but the continual rest that you are privileged to enjoy when you are in union with God. How I wish that all Christians would know this deep, restful union with God: to live in God and have God live in them!

2

Turn from Self to Christ

I have not forgotten you. God has written you on my heart.

If you have not accepted or invited the thoughts that cross your mind, do not be upset by them. Examining and dwelling on unwanted thoughts is what makes these thoughts worse. Do not fight with them, for they will draw you into a battle you, yourself, have no hope of winning.

Your Father wipes away your faults as easily as an earthly father wipes mud off a child's face. The worst thing you can do is to doubt God's love. He knows your heart and sees that you wished to do no wrong. It is all right to see how weak and helpless you are, but that is no place to stay.

Look at your God! When you see how strong and how able He is, then seeing how weak you are is not difficult to accept. Do not torment yourself because you do not always feel that you trust Him or feel His presence with you. Walk by faith and not by sight or your own expectations. Let us walk together closely—not according to what we want, but according to what God chooses for us.

3

The Love of God

No matter what has been said about my experience in Christ, I cannot doubt its reality. Somewhere deep within me I am utterly convinced that it is true. It is Christ at work in my heart, and that work is as unshakable as He is. It seems to me that these theological discussions concerning the validity of an inward experience with Christ arise from people who have not tasted so great a love. They are tempted to look at men when, instead, they should be looking at the Giver of love.

True, we are full of weakness and sin, but when it pleases God to transform us and make us one with Himself, we are changed into the likeness of Christ. Who can dare to tell God what He can and cannot do? Who can say that God, whose love is boundless as it is free, cannot pour out this eternal love on anyone He pleases? Doesn't He have the right to love me as He does? Yes, He loves me and His love is without bounds. I cannot doubt it! And He loves you, too, in the very same way.

This is eternal love revealed—the very heart of God expressed toward His beloved. When you experience God's love, you understand the mutual secrets that only the Lover and His beloved can share. Who can question it?

When I hold my Beloved Lord in my arms there is nothing to compare with it! In those moments it is impossible to deny the love I experience. I just smile within myself and whisper, "My Beloved is mine, and I am His."

4

Spiritual Progress

I rejoice in your spiritual progress. By progress I mean not going further up but further down! As when a ship is loaded, the more cargo put into it, the lower it goes into the waters; so the more love you have within you, the lower the old nature sinks.

Likewise, if you have a set of scales, it is as if the lighter side were the side of the empty old self, and the more heavily weighted side the love of God within you. Augustine said, "Love is our weight." Allow yourself to sink down under the weight of the cross and be ready to bear humiliation and suffering which are necessary to purify you.

By allowing yourself to be pressed down, you will find that this truly raises you up. Jesus says, "Whoever is least among you shall be the greatest."

I love you in the love of the One who humbled Himself on account of love. Oh, what a heavy weight is love, since it falls so far: from heaven to earth, from God to man! Give up everything to be known only by Him.

5

Streams from the Fountain

God reveals Himself to the pure of heart, and through them He blesses others that are receptive. These little streams which water others flow from the Fountain who is the Lord Himself. It is the Fountain alone that determines which way the streams will go. It is the nature of God to want to share Himself. God would cease to be God if He stopped sharing and revealing Himself through love to the pure in heart. As air rushes to fill a vacuum, so God will fill you when you are emptied of self.

The seven spirits of God around the throne are angels who come nearest to Him and to whom He abundantly communicates Himself. The apostle John was perhaps the best prepared of any of the apostles to receive the Word incarnate within him. It was on the bosom of Jesus—lying close to the heart of Christ—that John learned the heights and depths of divine love. It was because of this that Jesus, from the cross, could commit his mother to John's care. He

11

knew the heart of John would give her a place to stay. God communicates Himself in proportion to how much you are prepared to receive him. In this same proportion you are transformed by Him into His image.

How deep is God's love! He gives Himself to those who have made a place for Him. He becomes their end, their fullness, their everything.

6

Joy in Persecution

Thank you for your sympathy with my apparent hard times. God only allows me to see them as blessings. I believe that what appears to tear down the truth will, in the end, build it up. Those who practice and preach a deep, inward relationship with Christ will indeed suffer much persecution.

Nothing has any value but the love of God and doing His will. There is no happiness outside of Him. The joy born from giving yourself totally to Him no man can take from you. My only desire is to completely give myself up into the hands of God without any idea of turning back or of fear of what may happen to me.

And when I am in your will, O Lord, how can I be anything but content? When God's love makes you a free citizen of His realm, what power can imprison you? When God fills your heart with Himself, this world looks very small indeed. I love You, my Lord, not only as King of the universe, but for You Yourself. And I love You and all your people for your sake alone.

You have become so united with me that You are the Spirit of my spirit and the Life of my life. I have become so entwined in You that I could not exist by myself. If everyone forsakes me, You, my Divine Lover, live. And I live in You.

This is the deep well where I hide myself during times of persecution. How wonderful it is to be lost in God! How wonderful to be abandoned to His will alone!

How happy you will be when you no longer live by your own strength but by God's. Who can separate you from God? Absolutely no one can pluck you from your Father's hand. All is well when you are so united with Him.

7

Liberty in Christ

"If the Son makes you free, you will be free indeed."

When the *old man* of sin is destroyed and the *new man* is established within you, you experience a new and perfect freedom. As a bird let loose from its cage, you go out, totally free, to dwell in the immeasurable height and depth and breadth of God.

The old self life binds you in every way so that even God is not able to abide there and is deprived of what is really His. When Paul asked, "Who shall deliver me from this body of death?" he added, "I thank God, through Jesus Christ our Lord." When, by God's grace, Jesus is given His rightful place in your heart, you will be delivered.

When such a great deliverance came, Paul cried out in wonder, "I live, and yet not I. Christ lives in me!" He was no longer interested in himself, but in this New Man, Jesus Christ, who had come to live and act in him. He was steered by Christ, just as you steer the course of your body. If

15

someone else sat at the controls of your body, the body would obey this new conductor. This conductor would engineer the body's operations. Likewise, Jesus Christ is the life your new man lives by. And who is more free and more expansive than Jesus? His nature is divine, eternal, and without bounds.

So you can see how tragically you will be imprisoned if you cling to the old self. When you look at the freedom and spaciousness that come from living in Jesus, you then want to let that serpent of self be crushed underfoot by Christ. Then the life of God may (as in the first creation) bring you to life.

This freedom to be carried about on eagle's wings brings you into the heart of God. The dove that rested on Jesus was a symbol, not only of innocence, but also of freedom. Jesus gives your spirit the freedom to soar and dwell in God. May it please God to let you experience this wonderful freedom. Give your old self up and you will find unspeakable freedom in the One who is All in All.

8

Serve God Joyfully

I must warn you not to give any place to self-pity and depression. Although it seems quite natural to feel low at difficult times, a subtle temptation presents itself. Melancholy shrivels the heart. Melancholy makes it difficult to receive the grace that God can give. It makes problems appear bigger than they are and, therefore, too heavy to bear. Ill health and friends who offer little encouragement only make matters worse. You must see the wisdom of God's plan in allowing these troubles to happen.

There are two ways of handling little children. One is to give them all they want when they want it. Another is to give them only what is good for them so that they will grow up into maturity and not be spoiled. Your wise Father chooses the best way for you.

Having a sad face isn't going to help you, and certainly won't entice others to the faith! You need to serve God with a certain joy of spirit which shows that, no matter what

17

happens, you are glad to be His. Christ's yoke is neither a burden nor an inconvenience. If you want to please God, be useful to others, and be content; renounce your depression. It is better to divert your mind through harmless pastimes or recreation than to dwell endlessly on your problem.

When I was small, a nephew of my father's (a godly man who died a martyr) said to me, "It is better to want to try and please God than to be afraid of not pleasing Him." Let a desire to please and honor God stir your spirit even if it is just through a cheerfulness of heart and a happier face.

9

God's Care

I wish you would realize how much God loves you. As a painter draws on a canvas whatever picture pleases him, so God is now transforming you into His image through an inward crucifixion. He cherishes you as a mother does her only son.

Your Lord wants you to yield readily to His will even as tree branches are moved by just a faint breeze. As you abandon yourself to God He will take care of you. The more readily you yield to Him the easier it will be to know His ways. You will follow Him wherever He leads you. And if you make a mistake God will gently point it out to you.

God has the same right to lead and direct you as He has to possess you. When you yield yourself perfectly you lose your own shape, so to speak. You are able to take the shape that God wants to give you. Water fills the shape of whatever glass or container the water is put into. Let there be no resistance in your mind, and your spirit will soon lose itself in an ocean of love. Float easily and be at rest.

10

Do Not Seek After Signs

I am deeply grieved that so many in this present day, even some good people, allow themselves to be led astray by the enemy. Hasn't God warned us against "false prophets and lying wonders of the last days?" All true prophets have spoken in the name of the Lord—"Thus says the Lord." The enemy gains great advantage because people love extra-ordinary manifestations, signs and wonders. I believe the inordinate love of external signs is used of the enemy to draw people away from the Word of God and from the inward way of faith.

The signs that come from God encourage you to die to yourself. Manifestations that come from God will humble, quiet, and edify you. Elijah appeared alone among four hundred prophets of Baal. These prophets were all stirred up and were even attracting much attention by their loud proph-esyings. But when Elijah was told by the angel that he would see the Lord in Mount Horeb, he went out and hid in a cave, and he saw the earth tremble. God was not there. Then came the whirlwind. God was not there. Then there came a gentle, little breeze. God was in the still, small voice.

The only true and safe revelation is an inward revelation of the Lord Jesus Christ in the quiet of your spirit.

"My sheep hear my voice."

This does not take away your freedom or the natural operation of your mind. Instead, a beautiful harmony between you and God is the result.

11

Simply Speaking

I recently observed a man from whom I believe God wanted to rid the strength of the self nature. It is my perception that although what he says is true and comes from the inward work of the spirit upon his heart, his intellect is so powerful that it overpowers the gentle work of grace without his even knowing it. Therefore, some of the truth of what he says is lost. People are won more by the anointing that flows from a heart full of grace—by the weapon love—than by powerful argument.

Aren't the truths you speak analyzed too much by the intellect and further polished by the imagination? Their effect seems to be lost because they lack simplicity and directness. Like a song, they sound wonderful; but they do not substantially reach and touch the heart. There is no anointing.

Aren't you always looking for something clever or novel to say? Aren't you really showing off the power of your intellect rather than standing back and letting the simple truth speak for itself? Consider what I have said, and the light will reveal much to you. Am I speaking too simply? I only want to speak the truth and the truth alone.

12

Spiritual Fellowship

How close and how precious is the union of spirits made one in Christ! Jesus said so beautifully, "Whosoever shall do the will of my Father, the same is my mother, sister, and brother."

There is no union stronger or purer than spiritual fellowship in Christ. Delightfully, this is how the saints in heaven experience each other in God. This does not interfere with your relationship to God, but allows you to know others in and through Him.

Continually say "yes" to all that God wants. When you are united to God there can be no "No," only "Yes, be it so." And let that "yes" continually echo through you. This "yes" makes you flexible and agreeable to the will of your beloved Lord. When the angel appeared to Mary, she said, "Behold the handmaid of the Lord; be it unto me according to your word." It was the same with Samuel who said,

"Speak, for your servant hears." It was so with the Lord, "Lo, I have come to do your will."

I am yours in the fellowship of the spirit.

13

Different Seasons

The external actions of a person's life proceed from the inward man. When you live in your old self, you have a strong will and many desires, with ups and downs of all sorts. As your will becomes one with God's will, your desires are brought under God's rule and you come into agreement with God.

As you advance in the life of God, your natural, selfish actions are lessened. You depend less on how you feel emotionally, and you experience fewer emotional ups and downs.

Rest assured, it is the same God who brings both feast and famine, fair weather and rainy. High or low times, peaceful or troubling ones are all good in their season. These seasons form and mature you. Each is needed just as a year must have different seasons. Each change in your condition (whether it be an internal or an external change) is a new test to try your faith and love. It will help perfect you if you receive it with love and submission.

Place yourself in the hands of Love. That Love is the same although it may often ask you to change your position. Be careful if you prefer one state to another, or if you love abundance more than scarcity when God orders otherwise. If this is the case, it only proves that you love the gifts of God more than God Himself.

God loves you; allow this thought to help you see all your states as being equal. Let Him do with you as He pleases. If you are cast into the sea and are taken by the waves to His bosom or cast upon the sand (which means that you are left to your own barrenness), all is well.

As for me, I am pleased with all the Lord orders for me. I am ready to suffer not only imprisonment but death. There are perils everywhere—perils on land, perils on sea, perils among false brothers. All is good in Him to whom I am united forever.

14

Patiently Bear Problems

If my love could help comfort you it would, for I feel a tender sympathy for you beyond words. I am more certain than ever that God wants you entirely for Himself. Live in a state of complete reconciliation, as much as possible. Do not dwell on the coldness, temper, or contemptuous conduct of anyone. *The actions of others should not determine your conduct.* All that should concern you is glorifying God.

Endure your problems out of your love for Christ, who preferred grief to pleasure. Also, do not violate your conscience to please anyone. Consider your present situation as a way to show God that you love Him through a willingness to sacrifice yourself. Don't reject the cross (or should I say the crown). Let all this be settled between you and God in a quiet manner in your closet so that no one sees your inward struggles. As you bear the cross daily—and it is a true crucifixion—I am sure God will sustain you out of His great love. God is with you: therefore all that befalls you is equally good. God loves you; let this fix everything.

15

The Leading of God

You ask me how you can discern between the leadings of God within you and your natural thoughts and ideas. Unfortunately, there is no positive way of knowing! If there were, your transformation would become easier, assuming your intentions are pure. You must walk with God with a total sense of abandonment and uncertainty. You must risk making mistakes which are unavoidable when you start out in this inward way. Let me also say that if you are looking for some great, divine revelation for matters which your own reason and common sense can figure out, you set yourself up to be deceived.

The believer must act simply and without certainty, being assured that what is good comes from God, and what is not good comes from self. You will grow purer as the activity of self diminishes. Mistakes will happen less and less. You will more readily sense within you that which is of God. This is because you are becoming more and more an instrument for an indwelling Lord to use, so the self gets in the way less and less. Your Lord within you, with all His wisdom, is able to speak to pressing matters. He is established more deeply within you as you give yourself wholly to Him. "When they bring you before magistrates and kings, etc., it shall be given you in that hour what you shall speak."

Because God leads you this way—a moment at a time—it allows you to be free and unattached, always ready for the slightest breath of the Lord. This breath in you is like a gentle breeze and not a whirlwind that shakes the earth. Do not try to anticipate what God will communicate to you, nor try to know His will before you need to know it. After years of experience in this matter, it is my observation that God only makes known His will to you when He wants you to act upon it.

If you, wholly submitted to God, begin to do something that is not the will of God, you will feel a slight drawing back within yourself. You should then stop at once. If you feel no such warning, then go ahead and act, simply in faith.

A mother watches over her child as it walks; but if the child should start to go astray, she will call it back. This gentle calling in your spirit is just like the mother calling her child away from danger.

16

Dealing with Faults

Recently I realized how delighted God is with you. He has infinite plans for you regarding Himself and His glory. I believe I clearly saw the place to which God wants to bring you. I see, in some measure, how He is using the obstacles in your path. Since there is much mutual sympathy and trust between us, I hope we can always remain open and free to say what would be of help to each other.

You ask me about a "peculiarity" in my experience, let me try to explain. You say I do not seem to be upset when I am reproved for a fault. My reply is simple: I view my faults as though they were smears which my Father easily wipes away.

Do not think that I am blind to my faults. Living in the light of His truth is so precise and penetrating that it reveals the slightest fault. Those who are living in the natural life have faults, but nothing is being done to change them. Those who are being transformed by God have faults—

faults that are like writing in the sand during a windstorm! The wind blows them away as soon as they appear. This is how God, in His wisdom, works with those who are in union with Him. Isn't this a simple truth? It is so simple that the world does not understand it!

17

Quenching the Spirit

The other day, as we were speaking about how God leads, I was trying to explain something that you did not seem to receive. I immediately felt that because you resisted, I should say no more. What I learned from this is how gentle and delicate is the Spirit that wants to help others; and how the strength of man's freedom is able to oppose that help.

I also realized my own inability to help anyone. As soon as the Spirit within me is silent, I realize I have nothing to say. I am very grateful that it was the Spirit who led me, for I would not want to convince you of anything that was not from Him.

I now see how quickly that pure Spirit can be quenched. If we are brash or impulsive we can quench the quiet and gentle operation of God.

18

The Crucifixion of Self

All the graces that are produced in a Christian grow out of the death of self. Bear patiently the trials and sufferings which retard this overflowing life. When you suffer with much confusion and uncertainty, the suffering is even harder to bear.

Unlimited patience is necessary to bear not only with yourself, but with others whose personalities and moods are not compatible with your own. Offenses will happen while we live in the flesh. Bear these offenses in silence and submit them to the spirit of grace. Because you are human, you are still affected by your environment.

As you seek to honor the true cross (the affliction that God allows for us), remember that all the disagreeable situations that fall in your daily path are part of that true acceptance of the cross. Do not insult the work of the cross in your life by complaining about your problems. Welcome trials, for they teach you what you are and lead you to renounce yourself and yourself is, of all possessions, the most dangerous.

Give your brother my regards. I pray that God will strengthen him. I sympathize deeply in his troubles. I say that more out of politeness than how I really feel. I am convinced that encountering persecutions, and the loss of wealth and fame, are the best instruments to unite us with Jesus Christ. Everything, including things that appear evil, are great blessings when they unite us to the One who is our All in All.

My health still leaves me weak, but all is well in the depths of my spirit. God is there.

19

Correcting Others

It is important to be very careful and compassionate in correcting others. Speak only when you are alone with a person, and then do it only as you sense it to be God's timing. As you are not free from faults yourself, do not expect too much from others. Be humble and childlike and others will be better able to hear what you have to say. Jesus Christ was full of compassion and long-suffering. He patiently accepted his less-than-perfect disciples, even Judas, without anger, bitterness or coldness.

How lowly Jesus was. He "did not break the bruised reed." He does not rule by tyranny—neither should his followers. His people should use no heavy-handedness in dealing with others, but should say with John, "Behold the Lamb of God, who takes away the sins of the world."

The Lord "rejoiced in spirit" in a way that we find nowhere else in Scripture when He said, "I thank You, Father, Lord of heaven and earth, because You have hid these things from the wise and prudent, and revealed them to babes." How happy and relaxed we are in the presence of a little child, for a child does not instill fear in us. It is in this childlike spirit of meekness, compassion, and innocence that we should seek to help others.

20

Silent Work of Grace

I see by your letter that you question how grace can be passed silently from spirit to spirit without words. We see an example of this in the woman who touched the Lord when He said, "I perceive that virtue has gone out of me."

In a similar way, without words, you may communicate grace to others as God imparts grace to you. They must, however, be in a state to receive it, or else the grace will be turned away. As it says in the Scripture, "If they are not children of peace, your peace will return to you again."

This illustrates, as I see it, the inward communication of the grace of God between believers. Such communication is experienced in silence, and silence is often more effective than much conversation.

During our last time together I felt inclined toward silence, but you seemed to find this difficult, so I entered into conversation. Inwardly it seemed to me that it would have been better to remain silent, for I did not perceive that my words could help you. God wants to teach you that there is a silence through which He operates. This grace is passed from spirit to spirit, but is received only by those who are receptive. It is often more effective than words in building you up.

We find this harmony in nature. The sun, moon and stars shine in silence. The voice of God is heard in the silence of the spirit. The work of grace is silent, too, as it comes from God. Can it not pass from spirit to spirit without the noise of words? How I wish that all Christians knew what it meant to keep silent before the Lord.

Editors' note: In this letter, the author is speaking not of visions, prophecies or signs, but of simple fellowship of the spirit, believer to believer, and of the encouragement believers can be to one another.

21

Risk Losing Control

Let me urge you to allow your spirit to be enlarged by grace. If you do not yield, your spirit will shrivel and hinder the openness you should have toward everyone, especially those who are very unlike yourself. It is easier to win people's confidence if you are open and straightforward.

Do not think so much of yourself that you are not concerned with others. The things you assume to be your virtues, God may see as faults. You will not see things as He does until you have clearer light.

You seem to mark out a certain circle of friends and experiences for yourself. You are afraid to go outside of that circle lest you be hurt or lose control. If you insist on controlling your own life, your Lord will not force you to give up your control. While it seems that you are making progress, you are really only "going around in circles." Do you know what that circle is filled with? The self! I beg you to pass beyond these narrow boundaries that you set for yourself.

Allow yourself to be led by the will and way of God, not by what you want or think to be best. By doing this you will not only be happier, but more useful. It is because I love you that I speak so strongly to you.

Let God be the Master over your heart. Be open to whatever He has to teach you, whether that word comes directly from Him, or through others.

22

God's Work in the Believer

Do not think that you will be purified through extreme events or by great trials. What God is after is this: that you are always ready to yield your will to Him in a childlike way. By nature you are proud of your ability to reason, but God will often lead you in a way that is opposite to human philosophy. You must, therefore, become as a child with regard to your will.

What we call the "death of the will" is the passing of your will into His will. It is that simple. Your will must change, not only as it controls your external actions, but also as it relates to your innermost desires. Many believers who begin to follow Christ stop short at this point. They cannot submit to this inward crucifixion which cripples the entire, carnal nature.

When the self is left undealt with in the life of the believer, you can readily see how a religious monster is produced. It is possible for you to disdain worldliness but still be full of self. You may not practice what people consider to be obvious vices; but inside, the essential self-nature is still very much alive.

God accomplishes His will in your life by an authority that is gentle and effective if you fully surrender yourself to Him. As you agree to His work within you, you will experience the sweet, sustaining sense of His hand. God does not force you to agree with Him. Rather, He makes it so that you are able to follow Him happily, even across dangerous cliffs. Your Lord is good, and so is the way He deals with you. When you see this, you will want to run quickly after Him wherever He goes.

Be willing to give up everything to Him. This is vital to your progress. And remember, even this willingness is God's work in you. Happy are the people who yield to His discipline.

At first God allows you to follow what seems reasonable to you as you walk with Him. Later you learn to walk more fully by faith. He leads you as if you were blind, through unknown paths, causing you to enter into the wisdom of Jesus Christ. Along this sightless path you may begin to consider yourself separated from God and feel that you are left to act for yourself. Fortunately, to counterbalance this, you have, hidden deep within your spirit, the testimony that you truly belong to Him.

Human wisdom is of no use—it is only the wisdom of Jesus Christ that leads you toward full maturity. Once your will yields to God it will be content, for then your will is in its proper place. The crucial thing is to take care that your will remains there and does not return to its former way of controlling your life. Your reason, at times, may violently oppose your wholehearted submission to God. It may frighten you and entice you to turn back. However, once you have seen the useless sufferings your old self brings with it, you will allow yourself to be swept away on the currents of His love. After this occurs there is no more struggle, for you will be in your proper place before God.

True, sometimes this natural place of rest is so different from what you have been used to that you will still feel twinges of fear or anxiety. But when you experience what it is like to be a creation in God, you will see what simplicity, innocence, and enlargement is waiting for you. You become subject to God alone and nothing else holds any power over you.

Be assured that God does not invade the unwilling soul and overpower the believer. The turmoil you experience is your resistance to what God is seeking to accomplish. When you let go of all that is standing in His way you will find yourself swept into Him. This is what is called death to self; but this term is really a contradiction because when this happens your spirit can never be more alive. Your spirit then lives the true life, the life of God.

As your will is lost in God's will you still have purposes, but these purposes are God's desires within you and have nothing to do with yourself. God reigns from the center of your spirit, and everything that is not of Him dissolves in His presence. As you pass into fuller union with God you are changed and transformed by Him. This means your will is consumed and gives place to the will of God.

As you are made more Christlike, you begin to take on his qualities. One of these qualities is that of wanting fellowship with others who are on the same journey as you. It is somewhat like a stream which flows into a river. From that point on, it flows wherever the river flows. This river, which is like God, draws into itself all the smaller rivers (you and me) until all are lost in a great ocean of love. Each stream has no life of its own but flows to and from its origin. That is where you are going to find your eventual destiny: united with God. As Jesus Christ expressed it—"one in us." (John 17:21)

What reality is contained in this truth and how blessed you are if you understand it! Many people walk alongside the river but never step into the waters. But there are some who eagerly jump into the river and flow together in the fullness of God's love.

I am not imagining this! It is what God had in mind when He created us. Everything in the Christian life points to this glorious end: that we will be united with Him! Here is the light that ravishes the soul and floods the spirit. His light pursues you, slowly unfolding more and more as you walk more deeply in it.

This is the true faith, a faith of experience, that God teaches you as you abandon your own wisdom and embrace Him as your All in All. This is the law of wisdom. It is the way of the Lord within you.

23

No Fellowship
with the Superficial

There are some people who cause me great suffering. They are selfish and full of compromises, strange ideas, and human reasonings. Not only this, they want others to indulge and approve their ways. Such people want their self-love to be pampered. I cannot bring myself to do this. If I try, I am restrained by a Master more powerful than I.

Superficial relationships weaken the spirit. Rather than build up, they tear down fellowship between believers. Instead of the sweetness of mutual edification, there is only the clashing of broken gears grinding against each other.

The love that dwells within your spirit is not a natural love. It arises from a place deep within. Your indwelling Lord rejects all that is not of His nature. He expels all that is not compatible with the heart of God.

On the other hand, when you meet a person whose heart

is turned toward God there is a natural, or should I say supernatural, drawing between you.

Do not regard the external, but the inward state of people. See if they desire to be in complete union with God. The only perfect fellowship is the union of spirits in God. This union not only exists in heaven, but also on earth as the resurrecting power of life begins to transform the believer.

24

Do Not
Give in to Discouragement

Do not be discouraged when your progress seems slow. The process of dying to self takes a long time because self love is great. The self has many hiding places. It is deeply interwoven into your nature, and you have let it grow strong through long years of having your own way. Do not expect to be changed instantly. Be patient and let the task be accomplished a little at a time. Your progress will not occur through direct effort. Give up your own effort, remain quiet, and do not try to do it yourself.

If entering into deep union with God were as easy as walking into a room, many would gladly do it. The door that leads to life first leads to many deaths. I speak of death to self. It is this long period of dying to the old man of sin within you that causes all the pains of the inward life. It is rare to find people who are willing to die entirely to self; therefore, few reach the highest state of grace.

Be courageous. It is hard work to launch a large ship from her moorings; but when she is out in open waters, how easily she sails! When the self nature has been conquered through perseverance, you will know great joy. You shall find yourself in the abundant waters of grace! I pray that you will allow God to put His hand to the work. He will!

25

Human Weakness

I am delighted over our mutual friendship. I want you to know how happy I am to serve you in any way.

It is better to remain weak when God leaves you so than to have a strength that comes only from yourself. I once thought that the most spiritual Christians were free from faults, but I now see otherwise. God allows certain human shortcomings to remain so that you might be humble in your own eyes. Not only this, but through your faults He hides you from the fickle eyes of the world. The Tabernacle, which housed the glory of God, was covered with rather unsightly animal skins while the temple of the evil Herod was decorated with gold.

Do not be overly concerned about your human weakness and failings. It is part of God's way for you. Be as a little child. When a child falls, he cannot pick himself up but lets another do everything for him.

It does not depend on you, either, to make yourself more

aware of the presence of God. Let the desire to always feel the presence of God be crucified to the will of God. Take what is given you. Be like the little child who eats and sleeps and grows in a natural, trustful manner. God gives the best food for your growth, but it is not always the sweetest to taste.

26

Spiritual Progress

As you progress in your spiritual journey, you will not only lose sight of yourself, but of everything else except God. You will even lay aside any human ideas you might have developed about the Lord Jesus Christ when He was on earth. As you are drawn deeper into Christ, it is as if He becomes too close to focus on with your old way of seeing. This is because you are moving into more complete oneness with Him. Let all your old ideas go as God directs. If you think you are losing something by letting go of these religious ideas, then you will be encouraged when you find everything you lost and more within this deeper union with God. As God draws you deeper into Himself, you will experience these things continually and not have to strive after them.

When you are living out of your own life, you act as though you are the central reference point of life. But as you are united with God you begin to see Him as the center from which all things revolve. You begin to see how you are united with Him, and slowly you begin to see things as He sees them. This is what David refers to when he says, "Seeing light in Thy light."

May God give you understanding of what I am trying to say. I am not holding back anything, but freely telling you all that I think. To hold back even a small bit for self is like a fogged mirror: It obstructs the view of God. Seek to be clear and transparent, only what God wants. As you do His will you are made ever more pure and transparent. May God be all in all to you.

27

Spiritual Poverty

Do not compare yourself with others, for they may not be led as you are. God chooses to give some people brilliant gifts, but He has chosen you, stripped of everything, in the depths of spiritual poverty. When you see your total spiritual poverty and inability to do anything by your own strength, it brings you to renounce your self nature. Without this renouncing of self you cannot be a disciple of the Lord Jesus.

No matter what insight or revelation you have, it is nothing compared to seeing your total need of God. There is no greater revelation than realizing that you can do nothing of yourself. When a believer reaches this place, God takes everything from him so that he might have the Beloved alone. It is also a place in which you are shielded from the inroads of the enemy, for the enemy can reach only that which remains of self and not that which has been hidden in God.

God has chosen you for Himself alone. You are like the

innermost sanctuary, the holy of holies, which contained the ark of the covenant. The ark of the covenant is symbolic of the will of God. This sanctuary is a sacred place within you which the clouds of God's glory completely surround.

What a wonderful thing this poverty of spirit is, for it prepares you for the best gifts God can give. Do not measure yourself by how much road you have covered thus far; rather, measure with your eyes set on how much more there is in front of you. There remains a great road for you to pass over: That road is God, the Way. The more you enter into God's highest intention for you, the more I love you.

28

Spiritual Help

I could not sleep last night, praying on your behalf. I have an inward conviction that somehow God is helping you in our conversations together. So as He lifts you up on one side, He presses you down on the other by communicating His grace through someone else. This way of revelation is something that God designed for His own glory.

When you are just beginning your spiritual walk, God may use others more frequently to impart grace to you. As you mature, it is easier for you to receive things directly from Him. This method of His communicating to you is only a larger fountain overflowing into a smaller one, or two rivers joining courses as they flow to the sea. So receive this poor heart in the fullness of Christ's love.

29

Experiencing the Word

You ask why I do not use theological terminology in explaining the Scriptures. I do this because my Lord teaches me that while there is nothing as profound as the gospels, there is nothing as simple. Further, if you are simple you will express yourself simply. If you talk about something beyond your experience, you are bound to have a hard time explaining it. You will also be forced to refer to what others have said, and you will describe it awkwardly.

The Scriptures are written in a natural and simple way, but they express deep truths. These truths adapt themselves to your spiritual level. The Word of God cuts to your very center. It has a penetrating quality, and it efficiently accomplishes all that it sets out to do. No words of man can produce this effect unless, of course, they come through people that are pure channels of the Word of God. It is God's pleasure to express Himself and reproduce Himself in the person that has abandoned himself.

When God created man, He formed him from the dust of the earth—the lowest form of matter—in order that man might not rob God of His glory. Then God breathed into man the Spirit—the breath of the Word—and this dust became a home for the living breath of God.

As Jesus transforms you, He not only gives you a clearer understanding of the Word, but He Himself is the Word coming to life within you. Only those in whom Christ lives fulfill the Word or have the Word accomplished in them. Only they are able to interpret the Word. Mental learning is not the best way to understand and explain the truths of God. You must experience these truths for yourself. They must be born in you and then you will be better able to explain them.

30

Forget Yourself

I do not start this letter with a compliment, but I trust that you will expect from me only the simple truth that I speak as a Christian. I try to say only what the Lord leads me to say. You need more simplicity. The false sense of humility and self-deprecatory remarks that you present are not humility at all, but a refined self-love. See God alone. Fix your eyes on Him and never put them on yourself. Be pleased to speak humble, simple things as well as profound ones.

All our self-consciousness and uneasiness arise from self-love. This self-love can hide behind a very religious front. Lack of simplicity inflicts many wounds. No matter where you go, if you live in the old self you will carry your sins and failures along with you. If you want to live in peace you must lose sight of self. Rest in your infinite and unchangeable God.

The more you look at yourself, the more you get used to

looking at yourself. You return to yourself more readily than to your Creator. Turn away from self, and turn to God. Do not withhold from God the only thing He wants—the possession of all that you are.

Time is short; why spend it in the company of self? The single eye sees only God. You seem like someone who has been called to stand before a king, but instead of considering the importance of the king and how they might serve him, they are preoccupied with how they look. God wants to rearrange you and to destroy the self-nature. You are trying to preserve what He wants to destroy. Be more afraid of self than of the evil one. Satan tried to exalt himself above God, and this same attitude is fostered within you if you continually think about your mistakes. This preoccupation with your accomplishments or your failures leaves no room for you to be totally enamored with God alone.

31

The Ways of God

The way that God deals with individuals is almost as unique and mysterious as is God Himself. Aside from certain things that are common to everyone, you will have specific training that God tailors just for you. What God uses to transform your life may not work with another.

You will not be led into great trials that make you strong, but into situations that will reduce you to the helpless state of a child. Become like a child and be always willing to yield to your Father's plan.

Forget that you are someone to whom many look as a tower of strength. Run to God as a child who seeks his father's protection and care. Pride, a sense of self-importance, and self-reliance must give way to childlikeness and simplicity. Jesus says, "Except you be converted and become as little children, you cannot enter the kingdom of heaven." When will you learn that it is a sense of your own smallness, and not any alleged greatness, that God wants you to see in yourself?

Be assured that God sees and loves you. Please yield to those things that God is using to restore you to Him.

32

Comfort in Trials

I want you to know that I sympathize deeply with your trials. I present you before the Lord with all my heart. I pray that as you are called to take part in the sufferings of Jesus Christ, you will also take part in His patience and submission.

The Lord is always near you as you seek His will simply and sincerely. He will support you and comfort you in times of trouble. Bring to Him a calm and confident trust.

Jesus said to the blind man whose eyes He anointed with clay, "Go wash in the waters of Siloam"—waters that were peaceful and still. I want you to experience the abiding peace that Christ gives. I pray that you might become as simple as a little child. It is the child that draws nearest to Jesus Christ. It is the child He takes in His arms and carries on His bosom. How beautiful and how lovely it is to be as a child! May the sufferings you now experience make you childlike and submissive to the will of your Father.

33

In Christ

God has joined my spirit to yours in the oneness of His own nature. As you progress in this spiritual journey, you will realize how united we are in Him. The Father unites you to Himself by giving you His very own nature. This is what makes you His child. It is only because of this that you are able to impart any of His nature or comfort to others.

We do not know or understand how this help is imparted. In some people it is more obvious than in others, but it always adapts itself perfectly to the one who is to receive it. The gifts and graces of the Spirit may be easily seen. They also may be more spiritual and inward, depending upon a person's ability to receive them.

It seems that when I am with you there is only the simplest fellowship and grace that passes between our spirits. You do not experience any major results because you are not always ready to receive them. Perhaps if we spent more time together without distraction, you would see greater results. It is God's desire that there should be a mutual flow of fellowship between our spirits.

The fact that those who are in Christ are able to communicate something of Him, even if it is rejected, is a great truth. This ebbing and flowing of fellowship is like the waves of the ocean. During all eternity the fellowship of the Father and the Son with His saints, and the fellowship that His own will share between themselves, will be a fountain of incredible blessing. God designed man so that He might fellowship with him. He could create nothing greater than a mirror image of Himself. All the glory of the angels and saints is but the reflected glory of God.

God could not see Himself perfectly reflected in His saints without their having two qualities: the ability to have mutual fellowship, and fruitfulness. No one can be truly perfect if they are not perfect as the Father in heaven is perfect. They must have His very nature dwelling within them.

The people who belong to Jesus, His chosen generation, become eternal in their nature as He is because He dwells within them. The statement, "giving us His flesh to eat," is in reference to the nourishment He gives us as we have fellowship with Him. The eternal Word is the essential, undying life by which we live.

34

Spiritual Winter

Believe that I take a deep interest in your spiritual welfare. I certainly hope your confidence in God will not be shaken because you are going through a difficult time. In winter the roots of the tree plunge deeper into the ground. Likewise, during the winter of the soul you are plunged deeper into humiliation. Remember how confidently Job said, "Although He slay me, yet will I trust Him." Even when you are without comfort, stripped of everything, and feeling yourself as nothing, you can still rejoice in God. Even if the earth has no plants or flowers, God still exists; and because of this you can be happy. A mother loves to sacrifice herself for her child, and finds happiness in giving her all. Be likewise in your relationship to God.

When your weakness, sin, or inadequacy overwhelms you, come to Him as a child who has fallen in the mud. See how cheerfully He cleanses and comforts you. Can you doubt that God loves you any less than a mother loves her child? Doesn't He say, "A mother may forget, yet I will never forget you!"

Discovering your weakness and emptiness is evidence of God's love. Although this discovery is humiliating, it is also cause for thanksgiving. God can fill your emptiness with His love and grace. Times of emptiness remind us of our total need of Him. Accept such times with as much joy as if He were giving you bread.

35

Giving up Your Self

The death of self is not accomplished quickly. For a time, it is living death. Spiritual life is represented in Ezekiel's vision of the dry bones. First the bones were joined, then they were covered with muscle, then flesh appeared, and finally the Spirit of the Lord brought them to life. As you begin to grow toward God you will find many obstacles in your path. As you yield to God these things are overcome.

The river empties into the sea before it loses itself there. Each wave seems to encourage the river onward toward the sea. God causes waves of His pure love to wash over you and urge you on to Himself. The river does not lose itself in the sea until its own waters are exhausted. As the waves roll many times before they are lost in the sea, so will you undergo many changes before you are completely transformed.

It is a good thing to allow your self-nature to be crucified, for as you do so, God can take its place and become everything to you. Lose self and gain Him. Take away the finite and gain the infinite. This is a great blessing.

36

Do Not Depend on Man

What should I say concerning our relationship? I have no desire to plan either to see you or not to see you. Let God direct us. Are you trusting Him alone, or are you putting too much trust in Me? I am like a bruised reed and if you are trusting in me too much, I will fail you. God sometimes uses a person in someone's life for a season, and then they are no longer useful to Him in that relationship. If He wants me out of your life, dare I hold on to our relationship too tightly? God forbid. He may have designed this separation between us to cause you to give up confidence in anyone but Him.

Your Lord may no longer have any use for me in your life. I may have gotten in the way, no doubt because of my pride. I never implied that I was infallible, did I? Who am I but an erring person? Leave me, please, and unite yourself only with God, who will never lead you astray. People and situations are good only in God's order. They will harm you if you put too much faith in them. If God wants to separate us, submit to His good will with your whole heart. He deserves your whole heart.

Be humble and courageous enough to admit that you trust in people too much. Whereas unbelievers may be stubborn, God's people should be pliable in His hands. Whatever happens, you will always be dear to me in the Lord. Lose yourself in Him, and one day you may also find me beside you, lost in the ocean of His love.

37

Death of a Saint

I have a feeling that you will not survive this illness. I lose in you a faithful friend. During my time of persecution, you were the only one on whom I could truly rely. I feel my loss, but I am very happy for you. I could envy you. Death helps to draw away the veil that hides infinite wonders. Our Lord has strongly knit our spirits together. May the blessing of God rest upon you.

Go, blessed one, and receive your reward—prepared for those who are entirely His. Go. We part in His name, but I cannot say a final farewell, for we are forever united in Him. I hope, in the goodness of God, to be present with you in spirit at the time of your passing.

38

Fellowship of
the Saints in God

The assurance you give me about the union of our spirits
gives me great comfort. It is a union to which my spirit fully
responds, not in an emotional way but in deep peace. This is
true fellowship in Christ. It is good that you realize how lost
you are without Him. Your only hope is to abandon yourself
and trust in God. How blessed is this oneness in Christ
where all evils die and the only thing that separates us is the
frailty of our humanity. How wonderful it is that our Creator
has made a way for us to have fellowship with Him. This
glory shall be even more wonderful when all the evils of our
fallen nature are removed and we are forever lost in God.

In Him we are joined like little drops of water in an
ocean! How quickly do the streams join each other and flow
together when all the obstacles are removed. As we become
pure in Jesus Christ, the fellowship between us deepens, and

we flow together in deeper ways. Purity comes from entirely separating from the self and reuniting with God. If you want to, however, you can return to your old self; the choice is yours.

Our fellowship is independent of external situations and what other people think. In Christ we cannot be separated from each other, for we are one with Him; and in Him and through Him we are one with each other.

39

The Inner Flame

My spirit has been united to yours during my physical illness. As the outer man is reduced, the inner man grows stronger. Although God's work in you may not be as apparent as before, it is no less real. There is a secret fire that burns continually and quietly in your spirit. This intense and constant flame weakens your natural strength as it cripples your ability to do anything outside of the will of God. I believe this is what you are now experiencing. Occasionally, the oil of grace is poured on this concealed flame to give you a sweet and clear sense of the loving presence of God and what He is doing within you.

You exhibit two distinct fruits from living in His presence: inward retreat and a continuous "amen" in your spirit, which is a wonderful response to God's wonderful dealings with you. I am aware of a very close union with you. This union is not in the emotions and not in the will of man, but in the will of God. This is a fulfillment of that which our Lord prayed, "that they may be one, as we are one." Death cannot interrupt this union, but will place it more fully in God.

40

Advice to the Young

You are very dear to me. I pray that you come to realize that God alone can make you happy. Give yourself totally to Him, and never take yourself back. Love Him with all your heart. Retire to your spirit to commune with Him. Pray to Him simply and naturally without the use of many formal prayers. God loves prayers full of love and affection more than ones said out of a sense of duty. Tell God how much you love Him. This kind of prayer will soften your heart.

Do not run away from your required duties. You can be closer to God during your daily routine than if you shut yourself away to pray all day. This is because your Father holds you more tightly when you are exposed to temptations. Seek to continually keep fellowship with God. The only things you have to do are to abandon yourself entirely to His love and do all that is asked of you.

Do not be restless and impatient. This will mar God's

beautiful work in you. Rest in Him and bring to Him every-thing that troubles you. He will carry you as a mother carries her little child.

God will give you wisdom about what to eat and drink and about all the pleasures of life. He calls you to balance and moderation, and not to extremes. Avoid eating and drinking either too much or too little. I pray that the Lord will give you strength, wisdom, and comfort.

41

Good-bye to an Old Friend

Letter to Pere Lacombe (Guyon's Spiritual Guide)

I feel that I can no longer address you as my spiritual guide. It seems that the right thing for me to do is to detach myself from all earthly masters and follow the Master who is Love. As I seek to draw closer to God, I find myself separated from depending very much on man. I also find that the beautiful work that God is doing within me cannot be easily explained. Words cannot easily express the wonderful truths God has let me discover.

To speak and to act is the same thing with God. "He spoke and it was done." When the Word of God, who is Jesus, is allowed to work in us without resistance, God forms us into what He wants us to become. When Mary Magdalene was made whole, it was no longer Mary Magdalene, but Jesus Christ who lived in her that gave her life.

Paul says, "I live, yet not I, Christ lives in me." In the same way Jesus, the Word of God, is united with you.

How wonderful is your love, oh God! How great are your wonders! How marvelous is your work in our hearts! I am lost in the silent depths of your secret wonders!

But now I write to you, dear sir, to bid you a final farewell. Even though I will no longer have you as my director, I want you to know that you are very dear to me in the pure love which comes only from the Lord Jesus Christ.

42

God's Glory

What could we desire in heaven and on earth but the glory of God! It is necessary to desire the glory of God as He desires it. God, who knows all things, has a plan of operation. He does all things at just the right time. He waits until the right hour to accomplish His will. When Jesus entered this world He could have converted the world at once and destroyed all evil, but His wisdom did not direct Him to do so.

Listen to the Lord as He says, "My hour has not yet come." Do not interfere with His perfect timing by trying to advance it or hold it back. Fall on your face before Him and acknowledge your nothingness. Seek only to be an instrument in His hands; He may use you or set you aside as He pleases. Be totally committed to His desires, and indifferent to your own. It should not matter to you whether He uses you or not.

Remain in God's hands. He may cast down or build up. Let Him do whatever He pleases, both in you and through you.

43

Spiritual Union

Spiritual union between believers is a very real experience although it is not easily explained. To be able to truly help someone, it is usually necessary to have experienced something similar to their experience. I share the pain you are feeling, and this brings us closer to each other and to Christ. I see something of how He bears our weakness in this experience. I also have clearer insight into the quality of God which causes those that belong to Him to grow as He gives Himself to them.

I am in God, and He is in me. As He conquers me more deeply, He will not only draw me closer to Himself, but He will draw others through me. This drawing is more powerful than the rays of the sun. But never think it is the ray (which represents the believer) that is doing the drawing. It is always God who is doing the drawing. Seek to be a pure channel so that He might shine brightly through you. God passes on His nature through the atmosphere. So God imparts

His grace both through believers and between them. Their one common center is God. It is like the rays of the sun that find their source in the sun. Thus, believers are joined to each other in God. I realize that what I have said is difficult to understand. May the light that God gives you supply what is lacking in my explanation.

44

Live in the Present

Do not expect that the will of God will come to you in extraordinary ways. The most remarkable events occur naturally and without fanfare. It was by an order of the Roman Emperor that Joseph went to Bethlehem to be taxed, and Jesus was born there. When Hagar's child was dying of thirst, she laid him down to die, and God showed her a well nearby. See God in your present circumstances. See that He has arranged them in His providence for you, and submit to them. He sees the end from the beginning and plans wisely for His children. It is good for you to submit your ability to see so little to His ability to see all things in all places and in all times. His sight reaches through time and eternity!

Remember that the present moment is where we meet God. It is His moment; use it. Every moment He gives us, He gives for His glory. The present moment becomes the eternal moment of which we must give an account to God. Do not waste it! May God be All in All to you in every moment, both now and forever.

45

Give Advice Gently

A single word, spoken sweetly and humbly as Christ directs, will do more in correcting others than many words spoken out of your own wisdom. When unnecessary emotion is mixed with a correction, Jesus does not cooperate with you no matter how true what you are saying is. The person with whom you speak senses this and will not receive the correction but will be even more stubbornly set in his wrong. But as Jesus speaks through you, without the self getting in the way, His words accomplish much and cause the person to receive what you say. I realize that some may resist, even if they know that it is Christ speaking, but if Christ cannot convince them to change, then how will your zeal convince them?

It is important to wait for God's time to correct others. You may see a person's faults, but they may not be in a place where they would profit from being told about them. It is not wise to tell someone more than they can receive.

This is what I call "getting ahead of the light"—that is, shining light so far in front of a person that it does them no good. Jesus said, "I have many things to say to you, but you cannot bear them now."

The prophet says the Lord carries His children in His arms as a nurse. A nurse might wish that the child could walk by itself, but she is patient if the child cannot. Do the same and do not discourage the weak. Do not destroy good grain with the weeds by trying to weed too quickly! Who does not admire the patience of God? But how few imitate it! Even those who have received much grace still have many faults. This should make us all more patient toward each other.

46

Embrace the Will of God

During my recent and quite severe illness I thought about how Christ was willing to suffer that which God chose for Him. Within me I said, "I am ready, Father, to suffer all that You will." As I yielded myself, I experienced a deeper union with Christ. Inwardly I heard the Bridegroom speak, "I will betroth you to Me forever."

When Paul said, "I bear in my body the marks of the Lord Jesus," he did not mean any external marks on his body, but an inward bearing of the sufferings of Jesus Christ. In David's life there are rich examples of the many spiritual experiences of Jesus. Job was an example of one who was reduced to nothing, but later was favored by God and came to know Him deeply. Those who pass through a furnace of trials and suffer with Christ are prepared to wear the white robe. This robe is the wedding garment of the bride, the Lamb's wife. These people will become the dwelling place of the Most High.

Consider the example of the beautiful underground palaces we read of in stories, which are reached only after crossing deep caverns. Aren't these palaces like the inward palace of your spirit? These palaces are hidden and no one can find them unless someone tells them where to look. This fine house is where the Lord lives: "The king's daughter is all glorious within."

47

Helping Others

Your faults should not stop you from working to help others. Grace may operate effectively through you despite your faults. God reveals Himself through the more spiritually mature "fathers" and "mothers" in faith. Learn to trust them without placing too much dependence on them. God uses His servants even with their many weaknesses.

Although you may see what the Lord desires to do in another's life, you should not offer to help them except as God orders. On the other hand, when you are rejected by others, this should not stop your efforts if God leads you. God will produce the results He desires in due time.

It certainly is a great death to self to unselfishly release the work of the Lord. Do not step out of the path in which He leads you. When you mix your self in what He is doing, you only get in the way and slow down all progress. Your self-nature is so corrupt that it invades spiritual things and ruins them. It can subtly hide itself in many fine-looking disguises.

48

Death and Resurrection

This is no time to be discouraged. Of course, sinful desires will present themselves. Let them scream their loudest, as a child does when we take away a dangerous toy. Look to the One who dwells with you. He will strengthen you to bear these crosses. You will soon see resurrection.

The extraordinary peace you have experienced is the beginning of resurrection life within you. This sense of peace may ebb and flow because the new life is given little by little. Let me assure you, however, that soon this peace will fill you entirely.

As God has enabled you to embrace inward death quickly, despite all natural opposition, so He will quickly resurrect you. Let me warn you that after you are brought back to life, more loss awaits you. This loss of all the things of the earthly life will be deep and long. Actually, the death and burial which come before this resurrection cannot be compared with the total loss that comes after it. This is something different and puts you in a completely new state. You will rise from the grave as the bride of the Beloved.

The complete death of self does not happen instantly. It is not finished until everything of the old nature is consumed. Die to live. Lose yourself, and you will find yourself again. In doing this you will begin to experience the new life.

49

Inward Grace

While it appears to you that nothing is happening in your spiritual life, it is apparent to others that there flows a hidden spring of life within you. God does not give you a sweet rain which falls and covers the surface of your inward nature. Rather, He gives you a deep wellspring through which you live and grow and produce fruit ripening for eternity.

David said that the life of man was like grass that grows and quickly withers. This refers to the natural life, but also applies to the self-nature. The self is strong in the morning of the spiritual life (that is, when you begin); but as the heat of the day withers grass, the God of Righteousness arises in His warmth and the old life withers and is cut down. The righteous are like trees planted by the river whose leaves are always green. This is because the roots are well watered by the deep-flowing current.

God never stops working in you. Your calm, resigned state is proof of this. Take good care of your health; do not labor beyond your strength. God will reward you as you labor in love for others. These are labors which He always pays back. I pray that God will keep you for His work.

50

Give up Your Own Way

God has created you for Himself, but He will lead you by
a way entirely different from what you imagine. He does
this in order to destroy your self-love. This is accomplished
only as your purposes, preconceived ideas, natural reason
and human wisdom are entirely overthrown.

Self-love hides in many places, and God alone can find
them all out. You seek the honor which comes from men,
and you love to occupy important positions. God wants to
reduce you to childlikeness. He wants you to depend on
Him alone. Believe me, you will not grow in grace through
reading what people say in books or through human reason,
but from an outpouring of God within you. This outpouring
will reach and fill you to the same degree that you are
emptied of self. You are so busy speaking, reading and
writing that you have no time or place for God. Make room
and God will come in.

You speak of your many cares. If you give yourself

wholly to God, these cares will diminish. God will think for you and arrange by His providence those things you could not accomplish even with long years of planning. In God's name I beg you to renounce your own wisdom and self-leadings. Yield yourself up to God. Let Him become your wisdom. You will then find the place of rest that you need so badly.

May you read this letter depending on the Holy Spirit. Take courage and be assured that if God destroys the self-nature, it is only so that He might give you Himself. Seek to be nothing so that God might be all. When you are empty, God will fill you with Himself.

51

Conviction

Yesterday I spoke too quickly. I felt the deep pangs of conviction much like I felt when I first started my spiritual journey.

I couldn't tell if I had spoken too quickly or if what I had said led to a quenching of the Spirit. Something within me seemed to be thrown out of God, just like the ocean throws something up on the beach only to wash it further back into itself. I felt rejected in this way without any power to return to Him. I could not even feel regret at my state. I was willing to remain where God put me until it pleased Him to receive me again. I was willing to agree to anything He wanted. If I had been very upset that this happened I believe it would only have made it worse. My spirit, hidden deep within, remained fixed in God. He removed the more external fault that had caused tarnish but kept the spirit safe.

52

All Things to All People

I read your letter with great pleasure. Believers who are able to help others are those who are able to become all things to all people: to spiritually give to each what they need. Only those who have let Christ simplify them and make them childlike can communicate grace. These people can sympathize deeply with the weaknesses of others. They may bear the burdens of others. Sometimes they experience a great heaviness for others.

The book of Hebrews says, "You are come to an innumerable company of angels . . . to the spirits of just men made perfect." David was in the Old Testament and Paul was in the New Testament. Both knew God deeply. The nourishing, life-giving word is symbolized by the manna, but the reality is found in the Lord Jesus Christ, who is Himself the Bread of Life in the spirit.

53

Self-Knowledge

Accept the view that God gives you about yourself, whether it be an understanding of the fallen nature of man in general or your own personal faults. Do not, however, add anything of your own perceptions to this view. Continual self-reflection will not help you. It certainly will not remove your faults. I am not surprised that you have discovered so much evil within yourself, and I understand how overwhelmingly weak you feel next to it. As God purifies you, He will remove all that blocks the flow of His life within you.

The evils of your nature, which have been brought to the light, were hidden deep inside. Now you see them, as they are being forced out of their hiding places. Most people do not have so deep a knowledge of themselves. They do not suffer so much because they are not destined for so complete a death and burial while still in the body. Silently drink the bitter cup. This process will continue until you are in some degree perfected. After that it will become less and less, and then only at intervals until you are more completely dead to self.

54

Total Surrender

Intellectually, you can be aware of God, but you are only able to be lost in God by total and loving surrender of your will. When you have lost your own will in God, this is, indeed, the highest joy. This total surrender of your will into the will of God becomes a permanent state. Of course it is not forced in any way, for you freely give it up.

As love rules you, you become submitted to God, and you are brought into natural unity with Him and with yourself. The greater the love, the more you submit yourself to the One that you love. God's love does not bind one part of your nature while freeing another. He seeks to draw you entirely into union with Himself.

Your mind may think of loving God passionately, but if the will does not agree, there will be great inner conflict. There is a great difference between loving God with your mind and loving Him from your spirit with a totally surrendered will.

When you love God in an intellectual way, you may feel a sense of joy; but it is like water propelled by a sprinkler: It goes up with great force, but it soon falls back to earth. When we love God from our spirit, we see that it is like a river flowing to the sea. It is a river designed by the great Architect of the universe.

Love, which carries the will along with it, changes you entirely. This is the true rapture: to be wholly lost in God. This is what is called transformation: You decrease and He increases within you. I want to make it perfectly clear, however, that you always remain distinct from God; and you never lose your identity in becoming one with Him.

55

Abandon Yourself

The activity of the self-nature is the greatest obstacle to your spiritual progress. Refuse to allow anything to strengthen this old life. Watch out for applause; do not congratulate yourself when you have done well. Keep from thinking about any good that you may have done, so that pride does not grow and nourish an attitude of self-satisfaction.

Retire to your spirit as much as possible. This is done not by your own effort, but by giving up your effort and letting go of everything that worries you. Be quiet, so that you may settle down deep within, just as you leave water to settle down when it has been stirred up.

As you discover your faults and sins, make no effort in your own strength to overcome them. This is a waste of time! Rather, abandon yourself immediately to God. Only He is able to destroy in you all that displeases Him. I am absolutely positive that you, in your own strength, cannot correct the smallest fault you may have. Your only hope is abandonment to God. Remain still in His hands. If you ever saw how deeply corrupt you really were, all your courage to reform yourself would run away in terror! Because of this, God hides your completely fallen condition from you and only reveals your sins to you as He is ready to deal with them.

Rest assured that God loves you. He will take care of you. Have faith in His great love and mercy. You will see more as He unfolds it before you. Take courage in Him and all will be well.

56

Progress

When you first begin your spiritual walk, you may experience a very deep sense of your sinfulness and your need to abandon yourself entirely to God. This realization may bring with it much inward agony, and you will feel overwhelmed by it. Later, as you become more fully established in God, you may not experience these feelings so strongly, or you will be emotionally less affected by them. This does not mean that you have fallen away from your total submission to God.

As clear water flows, leaving behind it no trace of its path, so the states of your spiritual life may leave no lasting impressions. Rather than resisting or turning away from God, run without stopping into Him.

In my own experience I am no longer able to write about my spiritual experiences so completely. I have found deep rest in God. "My peace," says Christ, "I give to you."

I pray for the church; I mourn because God is so little

known and loved. These feelings, however, are passing ones, and I am ready to feel whatever He wishes. I am ready for anything and ready for nothing. All that is true comes from God, and all that is untrue comes from me. My only goal is to disregard myself and be received into God.

57

Prayer

After you have made a total commitment of your will to God, you need only to walk in that commitment. Give your King all that you have and then rest in Him. You need not keep checking to see if you need some major, distinct act of consecration to Him. If you should get slightly off the track, He will show you as you go along.

It is the same way with prayer. Pray very simply. When a request comes forth from your spirit, it will be received by the Lord as effectual prayer, even without words. From your spirit sense words and speak them. Prayer is then easily made. If the Spirit within you does not bear witness to what you pray, then He will not cooperate, and it becomes impossible to pray. As God takes the place of self in us, He prays for things that He wills. In this state you have no desire to originate prayers or think up clever things to say to God. Rather, you will love to be silent in the presence of

God. This experience is too wonderful for words. I wish that the whole world knew what it meant to keep silent before the Lord!

58

Inward Trials

I believe that this time of inward trials is so long because you are not only learning these things for yourself, but for others, too. God plans that you accomplish much for His glory. In your case He chooses to use inward trials that are known only to you and Him. I remind you of what our Lord said to Paul, "My grace is sufficient for you; my strength is made perfect in weakness." You will find these humiliations great companions for they will save you from falling into sin and error. They will prepare you to become someone that God can use.

From time to time you will find yourself once again in these pressing straits. Just when you think you are finished, they will suddenly reappear. The greater your humility and sense of nothingness, the more God will use you to accomplish His highest works. In this state of entire self distrust and humiliation your words will be clothed with power.

"I am come," says our Lord, "to bring fire on the earth."

Do not shrink back from the fire if it is already raging within you. You are a martyr of pure love—a sacrifice for the good of others. If you were less to God, He might spare you.

Do not hesitate to speak to me of your sufferings even if it appears useless. This is not so. If you speak of them simply you will feel relieved and strengthened.

59

Complete Rest

My desire is to give myself totally to God and to love Him far more than I love myself. Why would I oppose anything that pleases Him? How can I do anything but give myself completely to Him? Who could run from the reign of a king whom one loves wholeheartedly? "What can separate us from the love of God in Christ Jesus?"

I realize that while you are in this life there is room to sin and to be separated from God. It is also true that you remain in fellowship with God only through His continual mercy, and if He should leave you to yourself you would immediately fall into sin. Yet, I just cannot have the smallest fear that you will be separated from His love.

This wonderful assurance of God's protective faithfulness is certainly not something to inflate your ego. How I wish you would comprehend how good God is and how perfectly He guards what belongs to Him! How jealous and how watchful He is over us! Let God become everything to you.

See nothing, love nothing, want nothing but what He wants you to see, love or want. Let Him become so much to you that it becomes easy to love and submit to Him. Trust God as if you were blindfolded. Trust Him without questioning or reasoning. God is! This is enough. How great is your freedom in Him! Do not doubt that when all of self is taken away, there remains only God.

How can I have any interest in myself or claim anything as mine? What could I be interested in beside Him? How strange a thought! How unpleasant to think of possessing myself rather than being possessed by God. I am lost and hope never to find myself. God is.

60

The Depths of Love

I would like to reply to your question regarding your spiritual life. Be open, simple, and like a child. In the depths of your spirit be like a drop of water lost in an ocean, and be no longer conscious of yourself. In this enlarged condition see and enjoy everything from within God. Within yourself there is only darkness, but in God there is only light. Let God be everything to you. I have walked in this path for more than thirty years, although in later years I believe I have experienced His truths in much deeper ways.

Think of a bottomless sea: Anything thrown into this sea will continue sinking without reaching the bottom. God's love is like a weight within us, causing us to sink deeper and deeper into God. "God is love and he who dwells in love, dwells in God, and God in him." How deep is His love!

Jesus Christ is, Himself, Truth and Love. He has explained the Scriptures by fulfilling them; so when you are made complete in God, the Word is fulfilled in you as it was in Christ.

Oh, Love! You are the pure, total, simple truth which is expressed not by me, but by You through me.

Correspondence
Between
Jeanne Guyon
and
Francois Fenelon

61

Guyon to Fenelon

In the past few days I have continually prayed for you. These prayers are like a strong flame that cannot be put out.

Bear with me when I say that there remains within you some resistance to the free work of God's Spirit. I say this because the prayer of the spirit would otherwise not have been so intense. I have often felt this way about others, but I have never experienced a prayer so intense and long lasting. Please let God accomplish everything He wants to in your life. I believe that God destines you to become a burning and shining light to His church. Do not reject it through false humility or human reasoning.

God will use His own tools to accomplish His work. Because our spirits are united in God, our external differences and circumstances are of no consequence. How pure and simple is spiritual communion between those that belong to God. The Lord has made a way for us to enter into the fellowship of the saints. I wish that all Christians knew their high calling in Christ Jesus!

Let me tell you that the beginnings of the way of faith are very different from the end, when Jesus Christ, the eternal Wisdom, is fully revealed in you. I am certain, too, that after you have seen how evil you are by nature, God will reveal Himself to you in a remarkable way and set you apart for His glory.

62

Fenelon to Guyon

Nothing moves me more than knowing how ill you are; yet I cannot be troubled because I know you are in God's hands. Shall I come and see you? Do not hesitate to ask anything of me. In the name of the Lord I ask you to tell me how I can help you. Your last letter will remain embedded in my heart forever.

Slowly and with great pleasure I am reading your explanations of the epistles of Paul. I am especially interested in all that relates to the inward life.

I am often undecided when it comes to small matters. Sometimes I don't know what to do if there is no clear choice. There are often good reasons on either side. What should I do? If I follow my first inclination, I often find that it is a selfish choice; therefore, I hesitate to trust this manner of decision-making. On the other hand, if I hesitate and reason about something, my uncertainty increases. God humbles me. Each day I find many little things, too small to mention, which help me to die to myself little by little. It is in these small matters that I see those things which I seek to avoid, and discover the depths of self still left in me.

I am not really held back by any of these external troubles. While I experience some distractions, I also am experiencing an increase of sweet, inward peace, and a deeper sense of the presence of God.

The office of bishop may be conferred upon me. I may choose to refuse it because I feel that I might be more useful in my present position. Do you feel that this is a wise decision? Pray about this with me, and please let me know if God gives you any light on the matter.

63

Guyon to Fenelon

You are truly the Lord's, and He carefully watches over you. I know God will give you a strong sense of His will when it is necessary for you to make a decision. Given the present state of your heart, there is nothing voluntary that keeps you from knowing and following God's will. Distractions that you cannot help will purify you if you do not become too upset by them. Being aware of distractions is the first step toward a state of purity where you will have no distractions. In this state, which is still far off for you, everything within you is in agreement and acts in unity.

The reason why it has become so difficult to pray is that God is replacing your own earthly thoughts with those that are more in line with His will. God is leading you, not by the way of great crosses and extreme conflicts, but by making you a child. You cannot become too childlike. When you are a child, God will renew His image within you. You will no longer live, but Jesus Christ will live in you.

This is accomplished by the work of the Holy Spirit. The Holy Spirit will be like a devouring fire that burns and destroys all that is evil within you. Then Jesus Christ the Word will be formed in you, and you will be changed, from glory to glory, into His image. For it is written, "Our God is a consuming fire." I cannot now speak of the vast extent of this new life in Christ. You will discover it yourself in your own experience. I invite you to this wonderful life, which is reached only by the death of self.

64

Fenelon to Guyon

I find myself willing all and willing nothing. I will all that God wills, and want nothing of myself. This is what I truly desire, yet I find my natural desires and dislikes blooming like the leaves of a tree in spring. I am like a fortress under attack with all its defenses broken down. I cannot hide this sad condition from my friends: They see it in my face and hear it in my voice. I have no great temptations; it is only my weakness that gives the temptations any power. I have a hard time praying. When I do pray my temptations are great.

I do not find the inward fellowship and enjoyment of God that I expected. It seems to me I accomplish nothing. Deep within, I find a rest in God; but during the business of the day there is less of a sense of the presence of God and fellowship with Him. I am sometimes tempted to hurry matters to get beyond this stage, although I seek to live in the present moment and let all the distractions fall away. I am so spiritually dry and preoccupied with my duties that sometimes there seems to be no place for God in my heart. I feel distress at my low condition, but my desire to be wholly the Lord's gives me strength.

I am beginning to see that seeking the excessive enjoyment of spiritual blessings can be selfish and dangerous to spiritual growth. Spiritual growth can be held back by the very same means that previously encouraged it. I understand that anything that leads me to God, even spiritual exercises, are only means to an end, and they must not become what supports my spiritual life.

God uses my enjoyment of inward prayer, and of His presence, to draw me away from myself to Him. Yet if I become too attached to seeking these wonderful feelings and attempt to retire to continually enjoy them, God becomes jealous. They who amuse themselves with spiritual gifts and graces will be as unhappy as the man who seeks fulfillment through the natural gifts that God gives to us. Human wisdom becomes a trap. In it I find neither peace nor strength to win spiritual battles: It is a heavy weight to my steps.

65

Guyon to Fenelon

The most important thing is to give up your will to the will of God. God wants to lead you, and all He needs from you is your permission to let Him. In order for this to happen, you must allow yourself to die daily, moment by moment. In all the events of life allow your own desires, and the things which annoy you, to be consumed within you. As you disregard them, they will suffer and die.

This is the way of pure faith: to lose your will in God's. This will leave you with nothing to hold on to but God, and this is not easily accomplished; for when one prop is removed you find yourself immediately clinging to another. As you let go of some things, you may tighten your grip on others.

Aside from the basic way that God leads everyone, there is a specific leading that God tailors to each individual person. I have never seen two people so alike that they are led exactly the same way. These differences reflect each person's individual character and work together to bring glory to God.

What brings about the death of self in another may not do so in you. Your suffering, as you advance toward God, comes from your resistance to God's will, even though this will may not be understood at the time. This resistance, however innocent, causes a deep disturbance within you.

We must not judge how appropriate God's dealings with us are by how much we like or dislike these dealings. If you have lost your own will, you will be so well balanced that when the right moment comes to make a decision, you will be easily moved by God to do so. As God draws you into deeper union with Himself, He knows exactly what He is doing. An important step in your spiritual progress is to follow God amid many uncertainties. To always want to be certain of God's will is a prop, and it will hinder the loss of your will. You may not now be able to understand what I mean by the loss of the will. It is not easy to explain.

The more determined your will becomes, the more you will then be aware of your natural faults and shortcomings. This is because your will wishes to oppose all that is evil. Be encouraged: You are like the dying trunk of a tree. The tree may push out buds, but they will consume its sap and hasten its death. As you reach this state of death, which comes after an experience of complete poverty and misery, you will discover great truths. These truths are known only by those who are taught by God. Then you will know that God *alone* is truth.

I wish I could tell you what I now believe to be the plan of God in giving you His Spirit of truth. He will search you out and leave you with no possessions, not even yourself, in order that He might possess you Himself! In your emptiness leave yourself with God. Consider yourself the happiest of men because you are the weakest. God plans to make you the pathfinder of a peculiar, humble, gentle, and childlike people. Therefore, He will lay your spiritual foundation very deep. By losing everything, you will gain infinite riches and freedom. You will be eager to say with Paul (2 Cor. 12:10), "Therefore I take pleasure in infirmities, in reproaches, in necessities, in persecutions, in distresses for Christ's sake; for when I am weak, then I am strong."

66

Fenelon to Guyon

I am quite sure that no one can understand the depths of God's pure love except those who have experienced it. No one knows the depths of the Spirit of God but the Spirit, Himself. Until the depth of God's love has been personally experienced, this indescribable encounter will be judged with a very limited view. I am, therefore, silent. I am willing to wait until God chooses to allow me to explore for myself those bottomless depths.

I understand the kind of death that Paul expresses when he says, "It is not I that lives, but Jesus Christ in me" to be a condition where you are crucified to the world, that is, to all that is not of God. Then you will glory only in the Lord, and speak of yourself with objectivity, as if someone else is being spoken of. You shall be able to speak of the grace of God within and of eternal things because you dwell in God, and God in you. These are my views on experiences I have not yet reached.

Yesterday I committed a sin against a person who, by nature, bothers me quite a bit. I felt humbled by this, but it did not really distress me. I plan to visit him this morning to set my wrong straight.

67

Guyon to Fenelon

Recently I have had insight into the nature of spiritual union. How beautiful are your advancing steps as you see more clearly by the light of God! You have been created in the image of God. This image, now tarnished by the fall, is being restored through Jesus, the Word made flesh. As Christ lives within you, He restores you to again partake of God's nature and characteristics. In receiving a part of this nature you receive the power of communicating grace.

Because you are in God, and because God's nature is in you, you are able to have fellowship with other believers in a deeply inward way. When you are in union with God and are made a partaker of God's nature, you are able to communicate grace to each other, as God communicates Himself to you. Your spirit absorbs and reflects God's grace. This grace is able, therefore, to flow from heart to heart. Remember that all of this originates in God and is through God, and not of yourself.

God is like the sun, and His people are like its rays. It is hard to separate them, but they are distinct. Those who are more deeply united with God experience this manner of communication most often. It is God alone who draws and unites you to Himself and to others.

He may use you to draw others to Himself. The people God uses are people who do not stand in His way because they have been made pure and transparent. Seek to be a clean vessel for God to use; then you will be able to bear the burdens of others.

As you progress toward this deeper state of union with your Lord, you will encounter whirlwinds of temptation. But God's truth will win out. The ship, though beaten by wind and waves, will surely reach a safe harbor, for God is the captain.

I have found it difficult to find words to explain this experience to you. May the light that God gives you supply what I could not say.

Please read the fifty-fourth chapter of Isaiah and tell me what you think. I have opened to this chapter several times lately, and God has helped me understand how it applies to me.

68

Fenelon to Guyon

I have eagerly wanted to write to you since yesterday, even though I had decided not to do so before I saw you again. I always think of what a blessing you are because I see God in you without becoming distracted from Him by you.

There are no relationships that compare to those that are founded and established in God, even if it is hard to explain such fellowship.

I have read Isaiah 54 twice. It represents the glory and fruitfulness of the church which is, at first, a barren and abandoned spouse. The people that God chooses to use pass through a dry and difficult time where they are stripped of all self. This way is full of tribulation for our human nature. Later, when they are prepared, God enriches them and makes them fruitful in Him.

69

Guyon to Fenelon

You have explained in a few words the nature of spiritual union in God. This union exists very simply. It is a union that is not separated by space or anything else because it is established by God and is in God. I find you in God, and I find God in you. Our fellowship is always simple and pure.

I am not surprised that you sometimes have doubts concerning a unity of spirits. I do, too, but they disappear when I think that God takes great pleasure in glorifying Himself in His children, even the weakest ones. I want, above all, for God to be glorified—it doesn't matter what happens to me.

Just yesterday I questioned whether or not I had imagined an experience. Assuming it was His Spirit that was operating through me, I asked the Lord that someone I was with might experience a touch of God. Immediately this person, who was totally unaware of my prayer, experienced a definite touch of grace. She spoke to me of the great peace and joy of God which she had just received. Lately I have been impressed that God's love for His people flows from Himself like a torrent and blesses all hearts open to receive it. The love you experience and share with others is only a portion of His love.

Yesterday as I was sick in bed, I had a deeper understanding of the cross of Christ than ever before. All I could say was, "Accomplish your will in me." In this renewed surrender to bear any sufferings in union with my Lord, and for His church, these words came to me: "And you will be espoused to Me forever; yes, and you will be betrothed unto Me in righteousness and justice, in lovingkindness and in mercy" (Hosea 2:19).

Despite my previous conviction that I was not going to die very soon, I was so ill yesterday I thought my end was near. By evening I had a sense that I would recover, and with this conviction I experienced the Spirit of God greatly filling me. My heart was so full of God's love that my physical strength was increased.

I can tell no one here of these experiences. I know the Lord can accomplish much between us even though our personal visits are few. No distance or space in the natural world can stop the fellowship of spirits made one in God.

70

Fenelon to Guyon

I read with pleasure everything you write, and pray that you will freely follow God's leading in writing to me. Be assured, I will be spiritually strengthened. I already have been strengthened. I want to receive what you say. Please do not hold back what I now need, especially all that will help me to become as simple as a child. If you see anything in me that blocks the free move of God's Spirit, I want you to tell me plainly and without reserve. I only want to do God's will—nothing else matters to me. I know very well that my own wisdom must die, but all I can do is hold myself in the fiery crucible. God must strike the blow. I accept all that God ordains without holding anything back. What more can I do?

Will you do the rest for me with your prayers? I am willing to progress as God wishes, no matter what it may cost me. Whatever sufferings I may endure do not matter. "Sufficient for the day is its own trouble." He who permits will bring good out of it. Besides, I do not want to think what might be good only for me; I want to lose sight of myself so that God's will might be fully accomplished.

I am weak both in mind and body, and unfit for my daily duties, yet my spirit rests in God. I take time for rest and recreation. My times of prayer are erratic and consist of silent communion rather than prayers of petition. I pray most naturally when I am riding or walking. When I stay in one place to pray, my thoughts wander. You can judge, from what I have just said, how humiliating my experience is.

71

Guyon to Fenelon

I am glad that you are drawn more and more toward simplicity. I know that it will cost you much to die to your own wisdom, and no doubt for awhile you will often turn back to your own way. Act at all times in a simple way, not waiting to hear a special message from God or to feel an extraordinary sense of His presence.

Leave your spirit always open to God, as a room is left open to go in and out of as one pleases. While you must continually look to God for light and direction, you must walk by faith and not wait for extraordinary guidance. God will always be with you and teach you all things. He will give you the right words to speak at just the right moment. Inspiration comes in the moment when you need it. It is not the product of your cleverness. You must become as simple as a child who acts not by reasoning, but with a childlike faith.

Faith holds onto that which is nearly impossible. God

exercises your faith in many different ways. He withdraws the sense of His presence that has supported you and shows you how profitable it is to be rid of the self-nature. Later He exercises your faith again by restoring the sense of His presence with you. When these feelings return, He purifies them and expands the capacity of your spirit. At the same time you will feel an undisturbed, deep, inward peace.

In this way you grow and mature without losing your simplicity and purity. You will begin to experience more of the nature of God, who is one but who expresses Himself in many ways. You may not quite understand all of this now, but it is important. Sometimes you may not give in to God's leading simply because you do not see what God is asking of you.

God is great! He acts in so many different ways within you!

72

Fenelon to Guyon

I want to warn you to use great discretion with those who speak to you in apparent confidence. I also want you to know how much I have suffered because of recent scandalous reports.

Many thoughts have rushed through my mind and caused me almost unbearable grief. Everything seemed so humiliating. And I could no more dispel these thoughts and the grief that went with them than I could fly in the air. But as I held firmly to God and allowed Him to accomplish His will, I believe that I committed no sin. I believe God will make use of this situation to crucify my pride, my vanity, my ambition and my human wisdom.

I am once again at rest. My suffering on account of this scandal has made me reflect on the state of resignation to God.

You seem so unmoved by external affairs—even if they are troublesome ones. I have been afraid I would lose my reputation. My old nature screams at the first sense of loss. But it is good to see this weakness—I am afraid even of a servant, as was Peter.

Whether it is because of my poor health, all my duties, or merely negligence, I find it hard to pray or to make time for prayer (prayer in the traditional sense). What is even more strange is that I do not feel much regret at its loss, nor do I fear where it will lead me. I was never more exposed to temptations than at court and, therefore, it would seem likely that I should pray more. I experience a deep regret over my faults and yet, deep within, I have never been more peaceful and free, and never more childlike and bold in my conduct. I find myself united with God deep within my spirit as I pray.

I rejoice in the fact that I will see you soon. I owe you much.

With your help I wish to plunge myself deeper into God to discover Him and know Him in ways still unknown to me. I wish to lose myself in Him forever.

73

Guyon to Fenelon

It is true that I pay little attention to what takes place in the outside world. Evil reports are too common to alarm me. I knew you would suffer greatly through this situation. I also knew everything would turn out for your good. I believe that you not only have been kept from sin in the trial, but you have been purified, and your faith and abandonment to God have increased.

Rest assured that despite how weak and unworthy I am, God will not allow me to lead you astray or hurt you. I have known from the beginning of our relationship that it was God's plan to help you by means of one who appears so unsuitable in the eyes of the world. This very fact would cause you to suffer.

I, too, have suffered much. When I try to follow society's rules of protocol and do things only because they are socially expected, it becomes too easy to neglect to follow the quiet leadings that God gives me. I would not want to displease Him. I do not want to go against His will.

May the Lord teach you how close the union is between Himself and one totally consecrated to Him. If I try to think up a plan of action by myself, I become as helpless and weak as a baby. What I do must come from an inward leading—from the life of God within me. Each of us must pass through many deaths in order to come to this place in our own individual relationship to God. In this state, one does the will of God from an intuitive knowing of His will.

Note that there is a difference between giving up your own selfish interests and allowing God to act through you in whatever way He pleases. Very few, comparatively speaking, reach this place. This is because they do not have courage enough to die to the extent that is necessary. One who has come to this point has an abiding courage and commitment to do the will of God no matter what the cost. Such a person experiences a corresponding inability to do what is against God's will.

You will always receive strength from God when you need it. God will never leave you for a moment. He loves you beyond the ability of words to express.

74

Fenelon to Guyon

I have returned from the country where I have spent five days. I was able to enjoy the rest despite feeling a little anxious about you. I have enjoyed the things around me, but at the same time my poor health has caused me to feel a degree of indifference toward my surroundings. Through all that has happened I have found a deep union with God and a quiet submission to His will.

Nothing at the present time embarrasses me—whether it be my own faults, what people think of me, or the difficulties at hand. My faults are humiliating enough, but compared to the peace I feel in God, and the growth of my spirit, they appear trivial. I also feel this way about everything that I now suffer.

Everything seems to take its course so readily without my plans or manipulations, that I am sometimes tempted to believe that what I now experience comes from apathy and a loss of spiritual life. What makes this impression seem stronger is the fact that I have no burden to pray—nothing to pray for. Yet, I have never approached God in such a wonderful way. It is so childlike, deep, continual, and so much in union with Him. Many things around me try to tempt and capture me, but God turns them in such a way that I rest, or desire to rest, only in God. My spirit is like Noah's dove returning to the ark.

I had written you a long letter, but in the whirlwind of affairs, I am afraid that I have misplaced it. I participate in all your troubles and all your victories in the depths of my spirit. I needed to hear all that you said in your last letter. I feel that God is leading you, and is leading me through you.

I desire to follow where God leads, even if I cannot see where He is leading. I will follow Him as I am aware of His leading. This is still difficult for me. I am so used to reasoning my way along that it is not always easy to submit to the way God is leading me. But God is searching me out, and I believe I am on the right path.

I look forward to seeing you soon. Everything for God, and nothing for ourselves.

An Essay

75

Thoughts on the Inward Way

You are able to seek God in faith, not through intellectual reasoning or difficult effort, but by His love that draws you to Himself. It is to the innermost cry of the heart that God responds. At first you actively cooperate with Him; then you enter a state where He accomplishes everything in you as you simply agree to it, and great progress is made. At first it is very enjoyable, then it may be very dry and difficult, and finally, all is accomplished in you by Love.

What do you know about the inward way? It is to seek the kingdom of God within you (Luke 17:21). This kingdom is found in your spirit. It becomes necessary to stop looking with the eyes of your spirit at external practices and outward religion. Man, in his fallen pride, has surrounded himself with external reminders of his belief. But you must set your spiritual eyes inwardly on the Word of the Lord. It is written, "Seek and you shall find." This seeking is an inward activity of the spirit. It is a desire to find what is hidden.

As you truly seek the kingdom of God within you, this kingdom is expanded in you a little at a time. Inward prayer becomes easier, and God's presence becomes more quickly noticed and welcomed. People once thought that the presence of God was only in thinking of God. Therefore, one would have to force the mind to concentrate on God in order to find Him. This is too difficult, and one's mind cannot stand it. Thankfully, the kingdom of God is not found in the thoughts of man, but in the depths of the spirit. So all of this mental effort is of no real benefit. When you try to find God through your thinking, you will become discouraged. Your enemy, who fears that you will let God reign over you, tries to draw you out of your spirit and into external forms of religion. He tries two methods: by tempting you to earn your way to God through much work, which will choke the stillness of the inward life; or by stirring up the mind to pursue God intellectually. Neither one of these things will ever encourage the inward life of the spirit.

You may ask, "How can I walk in this inward way?" God sees deep within you and draws you to Himself, teaching you a balance in all things. By putting away all excessive, external practices, you begin to experience the peace of His kingdom.

Within you is your Guide. He provides for everything that you need and takes away the burdens that sin leaves with you. This Guide does not nourish your corrupt nature, neither does He forbid innocent pleasure. Your king is ever working within you in some measure. When you begin to perceive this inner kingdom, you may experience a deep sense of communion with God. This may be called the next step in your spiritual walk. Beloved Lord, I have sought You entirely in my spirit, where You have told me to seek You, and I have found You there! Day and night I have sought You. All my heart's desires are found in You, and now I have found You! Reign as my King! Establish your empire within me! I will do your will alone. I give You all the rights that I once thought were mine. I give You back everything that, in your goodness, You have given me.

At this stage in your spiritual progress you stop trying to make progress by yourself. You simply and lovingly behold God and what He is doing within you, without trying to stop it or speed it up. In the first part of your spiritual walk you actively tried to get rid of anything that might hinder His kingdom within you. This was often hard because turning inward is not easy at first, and your old nature is not easily convinced to give up its place.

At this point, you no longer try to fight any obstacle in your path. Let God do whatever fighting needs to be done. Say, "It is time, Lord, for You to possess your kingdom! Please do so entirely! I wish only to watch You!" This beginning of God's reign is wonderful. Days, or even years, may pass, separated from earthly pleasures, yet you will not feel deprived. You advance more quickly by this way than by all your previous efforts. You are not without fault or imperfection, but God's love reduces them little by little. God also does not let you become discouraged over your faults during this time. There seems to be no reason to fear, for you suppose that most of God's work is done, and you only have to pass into eternity to enjoy your King any more fully.

As you progress, however, you may see this uninterrupted bliss may pass away. God begins to draw you again. This time it is not only for Him to be all things within, but also for Him to reign within you without your having any sense of great joy. Now you experience the "exile of the heart." Deep within, you have a distinct impression that God reigns there alone. This exile, at first, is very painful, for there is a long journey between the time that you first seek Him inwardly and the time that He conquers you completely. This journey is marked by many trials, temptations, and sorrows. As you advance deeper and deeper, each step is marked by a purifying process. People often mistake the first step in this purification as being the last step! At this point, God wants to reign alone with you, separate from any help on your part. This is beyond any state you have experienced, no matter what you think.

When you have stopped your own selfish works, as the self-nature is killed, the defects of your inward man become more apparent. This is because God wants you to see what you are when you are without Him. As you enter this stage you will be troubled, for it will seem to you that you have lost all that you have gained. Worse than that, you notice faults within yourself that you had never seen before. You may say with the maiden in the Song of Songs, "I have washed my feet, how can I dirty them again?" You do not understand, beloved friend, that you do not dirty yourself in opening to your Beloved, for even if you did, He would remove any spot and make you more beautiful.

Meanwhile, it should not be your desire to become beautiful in your own eyes, but to see only how beautiful your Beloved is. As you allow this attitude to grow within you, and you really desire to die to yourself, you will be entirely happy with your Beloved's beauty. Yet, you must pass beyond even this because there is still a sense of selfishness in giving up your beauty to inherit the greater beauty of your Beloved. His beauty must stand alone—untarnished and unused. Everything must be left to Him. This is perfect love, which regards God alone.

I, Jeanne Guyon

by Nancy C James, Ph.D.

Guyon's books have sold in the MILLIONS!

This is the story of one who became the most known woman in Europe during her lifetime. Here is the story of her imprisonments more vivid than ever before. *I, Jeanne Guyon* will now spread the incredible story of her life even farther and cause it to be even more influential.

Now Nancy James has given us a new, better, and clearer story of Guyon's life. Dr. James has combined Guyon's biography and autobiography into one. The author has then cast the story in first person, that is, with Guyon speaking. Dr. James has added fresh, new insight into the life of church history's most revered and influential woman.

Jeanne Guyon has influenced the lives of hundreds of thousands of Christians. That includes Adoniram Judson, Hudson Taylor, the Quakers, John Wesley and the Methodists, Watchman Nee and the Little Flock, and just about everyone who has ever read her life story. Beyond that, *Experiencing the Depths of Jesus Christ*, which has never been out of print in three hundred years since it was written, is to be found on the list of the ten most recommended books for a Christian to read.

The Jeanne Guyon Nobody Knows

bv Gene Edwards

This volume is a look at Guyon's life that Gene Edwards discovered while in Europe researching the history of the Nonconformists. This included retracing the steps of Jeanne Guyon.

With camera in hand, Edwards photographed places Guyon's life led her - places never before depicted. You will find twelve pencil sketches of

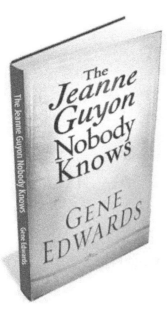

those photos included. These line drawings will allow you another visual depiction of her life. If you have been influenced by the incredible life and books of Guyon, you will come to love her story all the more. Edwards researched her life story to the end and found something shocking that no one knew - what happened to Guyon after her death. This is the first time the reader will understand what her imprisonments were like.

MORE BOOKS BY JEANNE GUYON

These are the books by Jeanne Guyon which have been
translated into modern English:

Experiencing the Depths of Jesus Christ
Song of Songs
Intimacy with Christ
Union with God
Spiritual Torrents

Commentaries by Jeanne Guyon:
Genesis
Exodus
Leviticus, Numbers & Deuteronomy
Judges
Jeremiah

Available from

SeedSowers

Christian Books Publishing House
PO Box 3317
Jacksonville, FL 32206
904-598-2345
1-800-228-2665
www.SeedSowers.com

SeedSowers

Christian Books Publishing House
PO Box 3317 ● 4003 N. Liberty St.
Jacksonville, FL 32206
www.SeedSowers.com

1-800- ACT
BOOK
1-800-228-2665

NEW	Author
The Jeanne Guyon Nobody Knows	*Edwards*
I, Jeanne Guyon	*James*
Here's How to Win Souls	*Edwards*

INTRODUCTION TO THE DEEPER CHRISTIAN LIFE

Living by the Highest Life	*Edwards*
Secret to the Christian Life	*Edwards*
Inward Journey	*Edwards*

SPIRITUAL CLASSICS

Experiencing the Depths of Jesus Christ	*Guyon*
Practicing His Presence	*Lawrence/Laubach*
Spiritual Guide	*Molinos*
The Seeking Heart	*Fenelon*
Intimacy with Christ	*Guyon*
Union with God	*Guyon*
Song of Songs	*Guyon*
Final Steps in Christian Maturity	*Guyon*
Spiritual Torrents	*Guyon*

THREE CLASSICS BY ONE AUTHOR

A Tale of Three Kings	*Edwards*
The Divine Romance	*Edwards*
Prisoner in the Third Cell	*Edwards*

THE CHRONICLES OF HEAVEN

The Beginning	*Edwards*
The Escape	*Edwards*
The Birth	*Edwards*
The Triumph	*Edwards*
The Return	*Edwards*

THE FIRST-CENTURY DIARIES

The Silas Diary	*Edwards*
The Titus Diary	*Edwards*
The Timothy Diary	*Edwards*
The Priscilla Diary	*Edwards*
The Gaius Diary	*Edwards*

DEVOTIONAL

Living Close to God (When You're Not Good at It)	*Edwards*
100 Days in the Secret Place	*Edwards*
Adoration	*Kilpatrick*

COMFORT AND HEALING

Crucified by Christians	*Edwards*
Letters to a Devastated Christian	*Edwards*
The Christian Woman Set Free	*Edwards*
Dear Lillian	*Edwards*
Suffering	*Pradhan*

BOOKS ON CHURCH LIFE

Climb the Highest Mountain	*Edwards*
How to Meet in Homes	*Edwards*
The Organic Church vs the "New Testament Church"	*Edwards*

OLD TESTAMENT

Guyon's Commentaries	*Guyon*

Genesis ● Exodus ● Leviticus-Numbers-Deuteronomy ● Judges ● Jeremiah

NEW TESTAMENT

Revolutionary Bible Study	*Edwards*
Unleashing the Word of God – with a DVD	*Edwards*
Christ Before Creation	*Edwards*
Story of My Life, as Told by Jesus Christ	*The Gospels*
Your Lord Is a Blue Collar Worker	*Edwards*
The Day I Was Crucified	*Edwards*
Revolution, The Story of the Early Church	*Edwards*

CHURCH HISTORY

Torch of the Testimony	*Kennedy*
Going to Church in the First Century	*Banks*
Passing of the Torch	*Chen*

BIOGRAPHIES

Shaped by Vision, The Life of T. Austin Sparks	*Beck*
Bakht Singh of India	*Koshy*
Against the Tide, The Life of Watchman Nee	*Kinnear*
Prem Pradhan, Apostle to Nepal	*Pradhan*
Madame Jeanne Guyon, Her Life, condensed & modernized	*Johnson*

BOOKS BY JOHN SAUNDERS

Modern Parables - the collection	*Saunders*

The Tiger Is Dead ● House of God ● Tabernacle of David ● Guardians of the Ark
● Heart for the Stretch ● Remnant for the House ● Kings unto God ● God of Preparation

EVANGELISM

Here's How to Win Souls	*Edwards*
You Can Witness with Confidence	*Rinker*